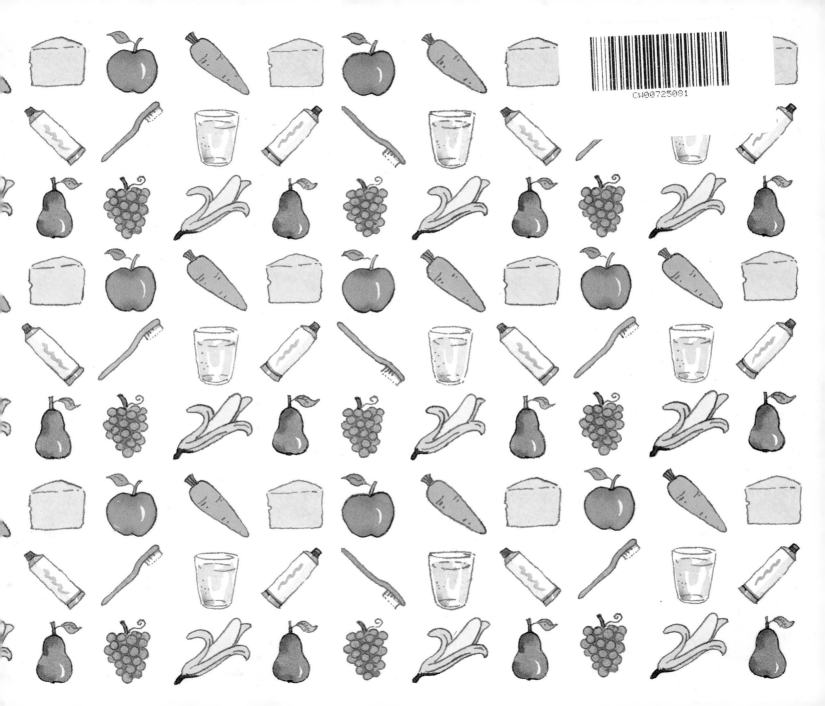

This book belongs to

Sophie Tindall

The author and publisher are indebted to James McCracken, B.D.S. (University of Glasgow), General Practitioner, Hemel Hempstead, and Diane Melvin, Senior Clinical Child Psychologist for the Riverside Health Authority, London, for their invaluable help in the preparation of this book.

Designed by Alison Fenton

First published in 1989 by Conran Octopus Limited
37 Shelton Street, London WC2H 9HN

ISBN 1 85029 225 6

Printed in Italy

Going to the Dentist

Robert Robinson
Illustrated by Nicola Smee

ConranOctopus

It's almost time for bed.
Mum is reading Danny and Vicki a book
all about teeth.
Tomorrow, they are going to visit the dentist.

The dentist isn't far from their home.
Danny and Vicki play all the way there.

'We've come for a check up,' says Mum,
and tells the receptionist their names.
The receptionist finds their record cards.

The waiting room is full of people.
Danny sees his friend, Matthew.
They play cars together while they wait.
Mum reads Vicki a story.

Soon the nurse comes to take them
to the dentist's room.
Mum comes with them.

'Hello, you two,' smiles the dentist. 'How are you?'
'I've lost my first baby tooth,' says Danny, proudly.
'You'll lose lots more as you get older,' says the dentist,
'and get new ones in their place.'

'Now then, who wants to be first?' he asks.
'Me,' says Vicki, quickly climbing on to the chair.

The nurse ties a bib round Vicki's neck
to stop her clothes getting wet.

'I like this chair,' says Vicki. 'Can I make it
go up and down like I did last time?'
'Of course,' laughs the dentist.
Vicki pushes a button and the chair goes back.

'How are your teeth?' asks the dentist.
'They're fine, thank you,' says Vicki.
'Let's have a look,' says the dentist. 'Open wide.'

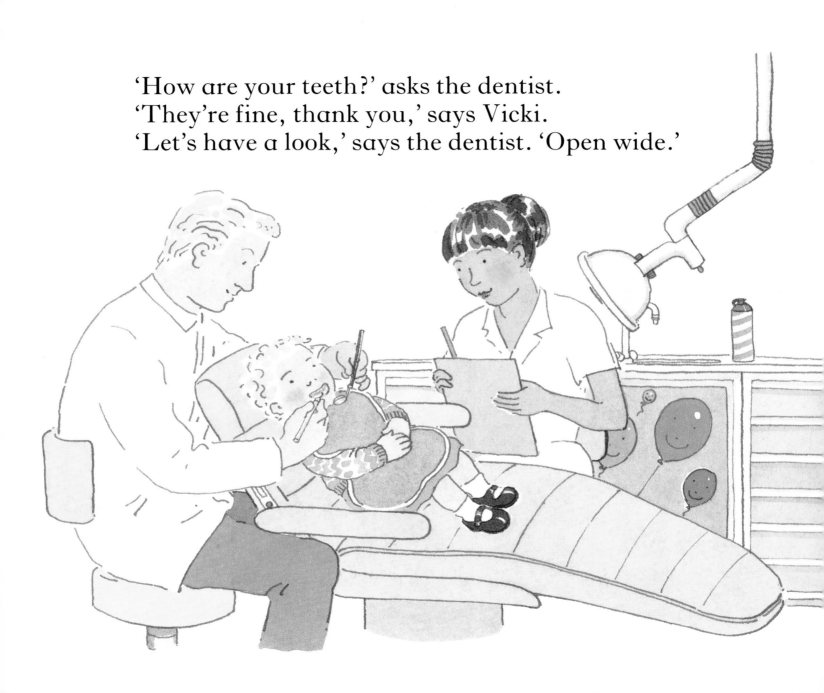

The dentist gently checks Vicki's teeth
with a thin pointed instrument.
He uses a little mirror on a stick to see the top ones.

'They seem fine,' says the dentist. 'Now I'll give them a polish to make them extra clean.'
Vicki likes having her teeth polished.
The brush tickles and the paste tastes of mint.

'Your turn now, Danny,' says the dentist.
'I want to see your new tooth.'
Danny gets on to the chair and opens
his mouth wide.

The dentist looks at all Danny's teeth.
He tells the nurse what he sees
and she makes notes on Danny's card.
'Don't forget his new tooth,' says Vicki.

The dentist finds a hole in one of Danny's teeth.
'I think you've been eating too many sweet things,'
he says. 'I'm going to clean out the tooth a little
with my drill and put in a filling for you.'

The drill makes a rumbling noise,
but it doesn't hurt Danny very much.

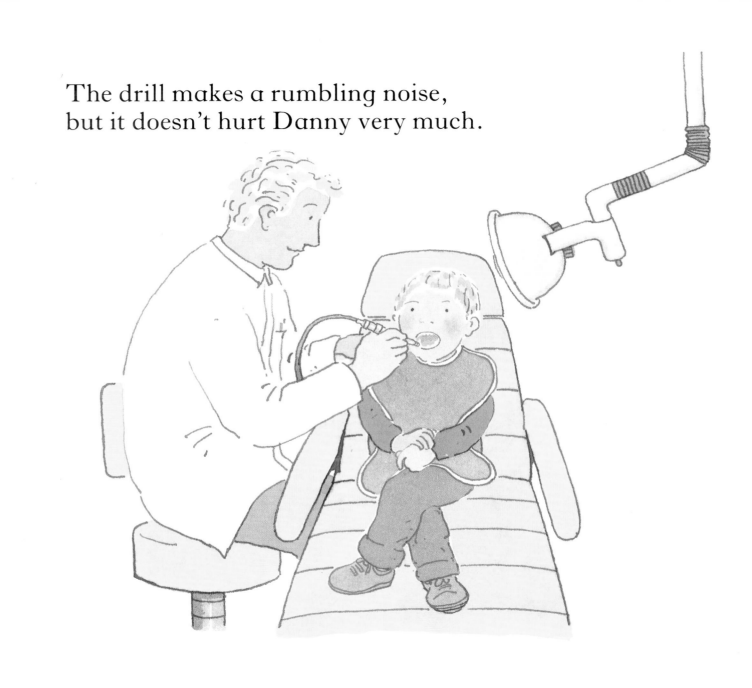

The nurse makes a filling mixture
which looks like cream toothpaste.
The dentist fills Danny's tooth with it.
'Leave your mouth open a minute,
while this hardens,' he says.

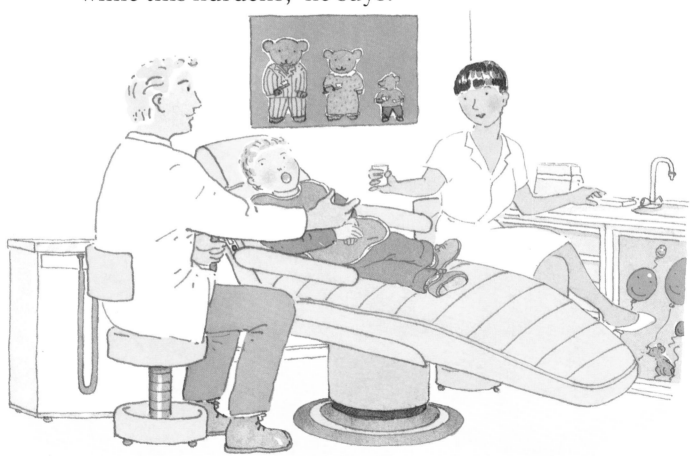

When the tooth is ready,
Danny takes a sip of mouthwash.
He swishes it round his mouth
and spits into a funnel.

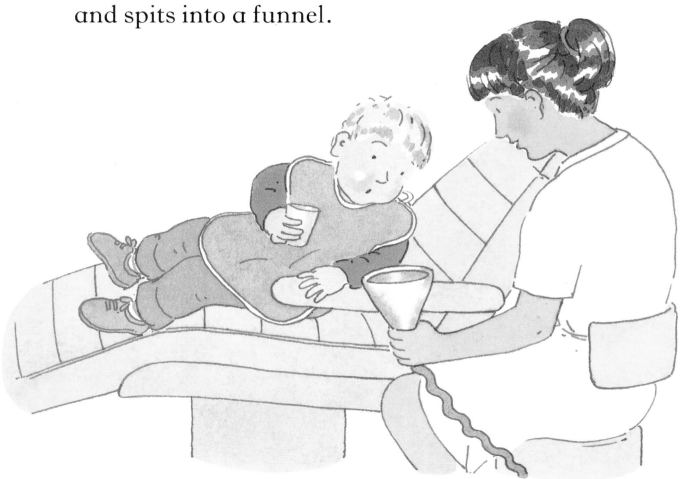

'All done,' says the dentist.
'Now remember to take good care of your teeth.
I want you to brush them twice a day
and try not to eat too many sweets.'
He gives them both a balloon and a poster.

On the way out, the receptionist lets Vicki
and Danny choose a badge each.
Mum buys them both a new toothbrush.

At bedtime, they use their new toothbrushes.
They clean their teeth really well
to remove every bit of food.

Mum puts up the poster in their room.
'If I eat what this says, I hope I won't ever need another filling,' says Danny.